HITTING
THE
BOOKS
Skills for Reading, Writing, and Research

Writing an Informational Essay

Precious McKenzie

Rourke
Educational Media

rourkeeducationalmedia.com

*Scan for Related Titles
and Teacher Resources*

Before Reading:

Building Academic Vocabulary and Background Knowledge

Before reading a book, it is important to tap into what your child or students already know about the topic. This will help them develop their vocabulary, increase their reading comprehension, and make connections across the curriculum.

1. *Look at the cover of the book. What will this book be about?*
2. *What do you already know about the topic?*
3. *Let's study the Table of Contents. What will you learn about in the book's chapters?*
4. *What would you like to learn about this topic? Do you think you might learn about it from this book? Why or why not?*
5. *Use a reading journal to write about your knowledge of this topic. Record what you already know about the topic and what you hope to learn about the topic.*
6. *Read the book.*
7. *In your reading journal, record what you learned about the topic and your response to the book.*
8. *After reading the book complete the activities below.*

Content Area Vocabulary
Read the list. What do these words mean?

body
chronological order
conclusion
contrast
descriptive
introduction
persuade
research
revise

After Reading:

Comprehension and Extension Activity

After reading the book, work on the following questions with your child or students in order to check their level of reading comprehension and content mastery.

1. *What is the purpose of an informational essay? (Summarize)*
2. *How would you organize an essay analyzing two different characters in a novel? (Infer)*
3. *Where might you publish an informational essay? (Text to self connection)*
4. *What is the purpose of descriptive language? (Summarize)*
5 *Describe the structure of an essay. (Visualize)*

Extension Activity

After reading the book, write an informational essay of your own. Choose a topic that is interesting to you. Follow the guidance in the text when conducting research, choosing a structure, and editing your work. Share your essay with your classmates or teacher.

Table of Contents

What Is an Essay?

What is a topic that you feel strongly about? Would you like to share your ideas with others? You can do so in an essay. Essays are printed in magazines and newspapers, on websites, and even in books.

There are many different purposes for essay writing. Sometimes we write to **persuade** someone to think a certain way about a subject. We write narrative essays when we tell about a real life experience. In **descriptive** essays, we share vivid details to paint a picture of an object, a person, or a situation for the reader. When you write to give information and facts about a topic, it's writing an informational essay.

Essay Fun Fact

The word "essay" comes from the Latin word, *exigere*, which means "to test or examine." Philosophers examined the world around them by writing long essays.

An informational essay is meant to describe, instruct, or explain. Think of an informational essay as a way to share what you know. You may not be an expert on the topic but soon you will be! Your teacher will probably assign a topic to you. As soon as you get your topic, it is a smart idea to start the writing process.

What Does Your Teacher Want?

Teachers have different expectations for each assignment. Should you use formal or informal language? Find out how long your essay should be. Does it need to be typed? Will you have to present your essay to the class? When is it due for a grade?

Keep a List of Your Resources

Sometimes your teacher will ask you for a list of sources. This is a list of all of the books and websites you used to help you write your essay.

Grab a notebook or use your computer. List everything you know about your topic. You'll probably need more facts in order to write a complete essay. Plan to go to the library, or with the help of an adult, you can use the Internet to perform **research**. You will need to find facts, definitions, details, and quotations about your topic. Your research will help you become an expert on your topic!

Make It Informative!

After you have gathered facts about your topic, think about how all the information fits together. How can you explain the topic or process clearly for your readers? What is the best way to organize your essay?

Say you are writing an informational essay about astronauts and their trip to space. You would not want to start the essay by explaining how astronauts return to Earth. It makes more sense to start with information on how astronauts begin to prepare for a trip into space. In other words, start at the beginning and work in **chronological order**. When you organize your information this way, readers will understand the process from start to finish.

Writer's Toolbox:
Words That Show Sequence:

Before	Later	Third
Next	Now	At Last
During	When	Finally
After	First	
Following	Second	

Another style of informational essay is cause and effect. Start by writing about an event, which is the cause. Then, write about the results of the event, which are the effects. For example, your teacher might ask you to write about the American Civil War. You would need to write about the causes for the Civil War and then find out what the results of the Civil War were and write about those too.

A cause and effect essay shows how events are connected. It is a good way to explain the relationships between different events or actions. By exploring causes and effects, writers can argue what effects certain actions may have in the future.

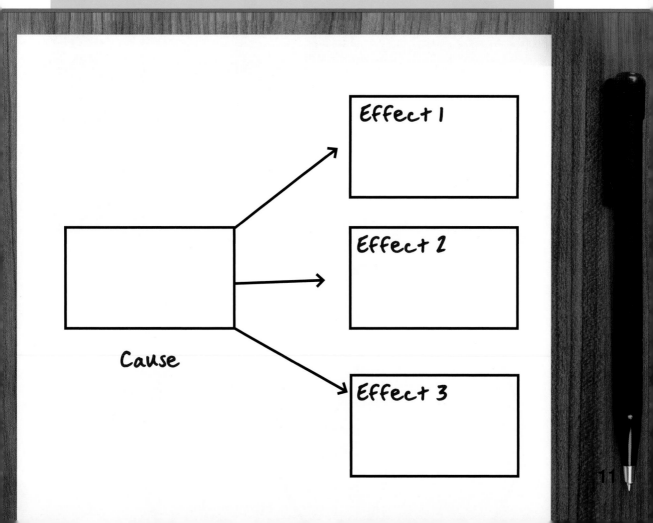

Writer's Toolbox:
Words That Show Cause and Effect:

Because	If	Since
As a result	Then	So

Or, you may want to compare and **contrast** two subjects. Say you want to compare and contrast the tundra biome with the desert biome. After you have gathered information about each biome, you would need to show how they are alike and how they are different.

tundra biome

both

desert biome

no reptiles

extreme climate

variety of reptiles

Find the right balance when comparing and contrasting items. The essay should not be about all the ways the biomes are similar. Explain equally how they are alike and how they are different. Remember, in an informational essay, you are not judging which one is better, you are just informing your readers of the similarities and differences.

AREA CLOSED
Tundra Protection

Writer's Toolbox:
Words Used to Compare and Contrast:

But	In common
Either	Similar to
Or	Unlike
However	As opposed to

Another type of informational essay is a problem and a solution essay. If you are studying the environment, your teacher may ask you to write about water pollution as a problem. You would write about the problems that water pollution causes, then inform your audience about possible solutions to those problems.

Describe the problem in detail. Then write about the solutions that could be tried to end this problem. Again, do not say which solution you think is the best. Only inform your audience about the solutions.

Writer's Toolbox:
Words Used to Show a Problem and Solution:

Because	So
In order to	Since
If	This led to
Then	

All informational essays need to be descriptive. Use vivid details to show what an object, person, place, or process is like. Make the topic interesting and memorable for your readers. If you are writing about Antarctica, instead of describing it as *cold*, you can use more descriptive words such as *frigid* or *icy*.

Try This!

Look closely at the images. What do you see? What is the climate like? Which animals live here? Brainstorm a list of descriptive words that would tell your readers more about rainforests.

Let's Talk About Structure

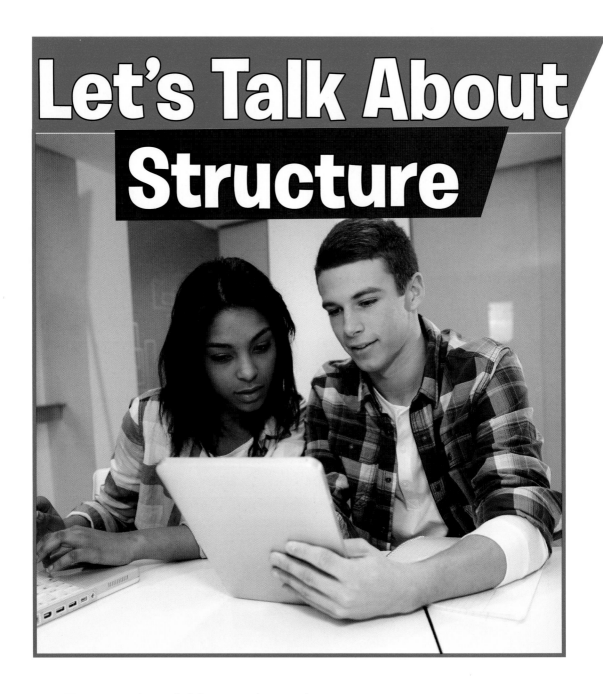

Essays should have three basic parts: an **introduction**, a **body**, and a **conclusion**. All of the parts work together to form a clear, informational essay.

The essay's introduction should introduce the topic and let your readers know what the essay is about. Start with a question or an interesting fact to hook their interest from the very beginning.

Honesty Is the Best Policy

Why is honesty so important in a friendship? There are many reasons. Honesty builds a connection between friends. When friends are honest with each other it shows that they trust and respect each other. Also, honesty shows that a person values what is true.

As a friendship grows, mutual trust grows. By being honest, friends share their personal feelings. Knowing that they have someone who will listen to their problems and not judge them is an important part of friendship.

As a society, most of us value honesty. An honest person seeks the truth and shares it with others. Being honest is not always easy when the truth can hurt others. But people who value honesty understand that the truth is better than lies.

Friendships built on honesty will last longer and be stronger. Being known as an honest person is a great honor. We all have choices to make on what kind of friend we want to be to others. Honesty adds value to you as a person and as a friend.

Honesty is ALWAYS the best policy, especially when it comes to friendship. Being known as an honest person is a great honor. It helps people establish great friendships that can last a lifetime.

The body of the essay is where you develop your topic. Divide the body into paragraphs of related information. Paragraphs help your readers make sense of the information.

Finally, wrap up your essay's main points in the conclusion.

Honesty Is the Best Policy

Why is honesty so important in a friendship? There are many reasons. Honesty builds a connection between friends. When friends are honest with each other it shows that they trust and respect each other. Also, honesty shows that a person values what is true.

Body

As a friendship grows, mutual trust grows. By being honest, friends share their personal feelings. Knowing that they have someone who will listen to their problems and not judge them is an important part of friendship.

As a society, most of us value honesty. An honest person seeks the truth and shares it with others. Being honest is not always easy when the truth can hurt others. But people who value honesty understand that the truth is better than lies.

Friendships built on honesty will last longer and be stronger. Being known as an honest person is a great honor. We all have choices to make on what kind of friend we want to be to others. Honesty adds value to you as a person and as a friend.

Conclusion

Honesty is ALWAYS the best policy, especially when it comes to friendship. Being known as an honest person is a great honor. It helps people establish great friendships that can last a lifetime.

Professional authors write many drafts before they publish their essays. They also have editors to help them. Use your friends to help you edit your drafts. Take their advice and **revise** your essay. Return the favor and help them revise their drafts. With teamwork, you can write like a pro!

Publish It!

Share your essay with your class on a blog, website, or in a newsletter.

Glossary

body (BOD-ee): the main part of an essay

chronological order (kron-uh-LOJ-uh-kuhl OR-dur): arranged in the order that the events happened

conclusion (kuhn-KLOO-shuhn): the ending of an essay

contrast (kon-trast): to find the differences between things

descriptive (di-SKRIPT-iv): using words to create powerful images

introduction (in-truh-DUHK-shuhn): the beginning of an essay

persuade (pur-SWADE): making someone do or believe things by giving convincing reasons

research (ri-SURCH): to find out more about a topic by reading

revise (ri-VIZE): to change writing to make it correct or better

Index

Websites to Visit

http://www.ala.org/aasl/aboutaasl/aaslcommunity/quicklinks/k12students
/aaslkctools

http://kids.usa.gov/reading-and-writing/index.shtml

http://pbskids.org/writerscontest/

About the Author

Precious McKenzie lives in Billings, Montana. She teaches college students how to perform research and write long essays. In her free time, she likes to read books and ride horses.

Meet The Author!
www.meetREMauthors.com

www.rourkeeducationalmedia.com

PHOTO CREDITS: Cover © jane; title page © Goodluz, Andrey Kuzmin; page 3 © Sorendis; page 4 © Wavebreak Media LTD; page 5 © Tarzhanova, Antonio Abrignani; page 6 © Rob Marmion, Carolyn Franks; page 7 © asiseeit; page 8 © mattjeacock; page 9 © 1971yes, Craoloyn Franks; page 10 © Library of Congress; page 11 © Carolyn Franks, Perssureua; page 12 © Sergei Uriadnikov, Ferli Achivulli; page 13 © Picasa 2.6, Laborant, Carolyn Franks; page 14 Over Crew; page 15 © Carolyn Franks, Antonio Gullen; page 16 © staphy; page 17 © Andrey Kuzmin, Oleksly Mark, Brandon Alms, Welcomia, rustyphil, Volodimir Kalina; page 18 © Goodluz; page 19, 20 © Bonerok; page 21 © michaeljung

Edited by: Jill Sherman

Cover and Interior Design by: Jen Thomas

Library of Congress PCN Data

Writing an Informational Essay / Precious McKenzie
(Hitting the Books: Skills for Reading, Writing, and Research)
ISBN (hard cover) 978-1-62717-692-7 (alk. paper)
ISBN (soft cover) 978-1-62717-814-3
ISBN (e-Book) 978-1-62717-929-4
Library of Congress Control Number: 2014935486

Rourke Educational Media
Printed in the United States of America,
North Mankato, Minnesota

Also Available as:
ROURKE'S
e-Books